RUBAIYAT-E-SARMAD
POET AND MARTYR

Selected and Translated by

Mahmood Jamal

First published by Farida Jamal 2021

faridafjamal@gmail.com

Cover design: Mahmood Jamal

MAHMOOD JAMAL was born in Lucknow, India, in 1948. He came to Britain from Pakistan in 1967. In 1984, Mahmood Jamal was the recipient of the Minority Rights Group Award for his poetry, translations and critical writings. In the same year, he published his first volume of poetry, Silence Inside a Gun's Mouth. Mahmood Jamal worked as an independent producer and writer and produced several documentary series, notably a series on Islam entitled Islamic Conversations. He was also a lead writer on Britain's first Asian soap, Family Pride, and wrote and produced the ground-breaking drama Turning World for Channel 4 television. He was the author of several books of translations, namely Penguin Book of Modern Urdu Poetry (1986), Islamic Mystical Poetry (2009) and Faiz 50 Poems (2011). He was the Writer and Producer of *RAHM (MERCY)*, a feature film based on William Shakespeare's *MEASURE FOR MEASURE* set in Lahore.

Published Works

COINS FOR CHARON (Courtfield Press, 1976)

SILENCE INSIDE A GUN'S MOUTH (Kala Press, London, 1984)

PENGUIN BOOK OF MODERN URDU POETRY (Penguin Books, London, 1986)

MODERN URDU POETRY (Farida Jamal/Translit, Kuala Lumpur, 1995)

SONG OF THE FLUTE (Culture House, London, 2000)

SUGAR-COATED PILL (Wordpower Edinburgh, 2007)

ISLAMIC MYSTICAL POETRY (Penguin, London, 2009)

FAIZ FIFTY POEMS (OUP Karachi, 2011)

GANDHI'S URDU LETTERS: THE MAULANA AND THE MAHATMA (eBook, Ideaindia.com, London, 2011)

THE DREAM AND OTHER POEMS (Amazon, 2020)

STARS (Amazon, 2020)

Anthologies in which poems have appeared:

ANGELS OF FIRE (Chatto and Windus, 1986)

NEW BRITISH POETRY (Paladin Books, 1988)

GRANDCHILDREN OF ALBION (New Departures, 1992)

THE REPUBLIC OF CONSCIENCE (Aird Books, 1992)

VOICES OF CONSCIENCE (Iron Press, 1995)

POW (New Departures, 1996)

POP! (New Departures)

VELOCITY (Apples & Snakes, 2003)

GARGOYLE (Paycock Press, 1997)

RANTERS, RAVERS AND RHYMERS (Collins, 1990)

RAINBOW WORLD (Hodder Wayland, 2003)

CONTENTS

PREFACE

Sarmad, the poet was executed for blasphemy, by the Mughal Emperor, Aurangzeb in the year 1661AD. He had, to put it mildly, an eventful life and a tragic end. Of Armenian origin, he had converted to Islam and came to Sindh from Iran to trade, as was very common at the time; and while he was travelling in Sindh, in a town called Thatta, he fell in love with a Brahmin youth and never quite recovered his composure after that. In keeping with the *Sufi* ideal of progression to Truth through love, he became a wandering poet and *dervish*, abandoning his trade and even his garments. He arrived in Delhi of the time when an intense battle for power was taking place between Aurangzeb and Dara Shikoh who were

1

rivals to Emperor Shah Jahan's throne. On arrival in Delhi, Sarmad acquired a reputation for his poetry and sayings and as a man of wisdom and knowledge and was courted by Dara Shikoh, who had a reputation of entertaining and meeting with *dervishes* and *Sufis*. Whether intentionally or inadvertently, he got involved in the battle between these two sons of Shah Jahan and paid the price of being an associate and well-wisher of Dara Shikoh, who was defeated and executed by Aurangzeb. Soon after, Sarmad too was tried and convicted for blasphemy and executed by Aurangzeb in 1661. Because of the nature of his life and his tragic end, a lot has been written about his life and martyrdom, but his reputation as a poet has not been assessed in the literary sense. What remains in the main of Sarmad's poetry are his *rubaiyat* or quatrains.

I first came to appreciate Sarmad's intriguing and sometimes rebellious *rubaiyat* through my family history. My grandfather, Maulana Abdul Bari Firangi Mahali (d 1926), quoted a *rubai* of Sarmad as a comment on his relationship with Gandhiji during the non-cooperation and Khilafat movement in 1920s. It was an ironic and witty way of silencing his critics:

2

Sarmad dar deen ajab shikaste kardi
Imaan ba fida-e chashme maste kardi
Umraist ke ayaat o ahadith giraft
Rafti o nisaar e butt paraste kardi.

(Sarmad, what havoc on religion you have bestowed/ You've sacrificed belief for a pair of languid eyes/ Having spent your life on *hadith* and the Quran divine/ You went, and to that idol-worshipper your life consigned!)

Then later, my father, Maulana Jamal Mian (d 2012), speaking on All India Radio immediately after Gandhiji's assassination in 1948, and paying tribute to him, quoted Sarmad again:

Sarmad gham-e Ishq bul havas ra na dihand
Soz-e dil-e parvana magas ra na dihand
Umre bayad ke yaar ayad ba kinaar
Een Daulat-e Sarmad hama kas ra na dihand.

(Sarmad, the sorrow of love is not given to the pleasure seeker/ The burning of the moth is not given to the bee/ It takes a lifetime for the Beloved to come in your embrace/ This wealth and fortune do not come to all and sundry)

3

Apart from the above two *rubais* (quatrains) and a couple of ghazals, I heard during *qawwali* sessions, I knew little about Sarmad's poetry till a friend in London lent me a book which had most of Sarmad's *rubaiyat*. Further it had an enthralling, poetic and mystical essay entitled 'Sarmad Shaheed' by Maulana Abul Kalam Azad (1888-1858). I read the book with keen interest and got familiar with not only the details of Sarmad's life, but also his poetry. Since then, I have been fascinated by his poetry and over the last few years, I decided to translate RUBAIYAT-E-SARMAD bit by bit with help from my brother, Ahmad Abdul Bari, and now I have enough translations under my belt to produce this book. This is a representative selection though, not all his *rubais*.

My approach to this book has been to introduce Sarmad and his *rubaiyat* to an English-speaking audience, something akin to Fitzgerald's Rubaiyat of Umar Khayyam, but more faithful to, and taking less liberties with the original! I have not used parallel Persian text deliberately, partly to recreate the original in English for English readers and partly to make it a convenient publication from typesetting point of view. I see each *rubai* (quatrain) as a stand-alone poem.

4

Sarmad has gone down in Indian history as a martyr and is celebrated in *Sufi* circles in South Asia as a true lover of God and an innocent man, unjustly killed for blasphemy. Most agree, however, that this was done because of political intrigue rather than demands of *Sharia*, as we shall see from Maulana Azad's excellent essay translated by me from Urdu and reproduced below. Apart from being a masterpiece of Urdu literature, this essay, first published in 1910 is a manifesto of Humanist and Enlightened Islam – hence its relevance to our times. It has been printed and reprinted in Urdu many times since it first appeared, but I feel it is time for it to reach a wider audience.

Mahmood Jamal 2020

SARMAD *SHAHEED* (THE MARTYR)
by

Maulana Abul Kalam Azad

Those who have chosen Your Love
Find their place of rest in the street of
Martyrdom
Love is victorious in the battle between the two
worlds
Though its whole army is martyred in this
field.

Of all the histories written since the time of Aurangzeb, the last Moghul Emperor of India, we get perhaps only a few lines on the subject of Sarmad. The problem is that, firstly, the old *TAZKIRAS* are generally inadequate and are often briefer than an address written on an envelope and furthermore, the ones that do exist are unavailable to me. I have searched the histories written during Aurangzeb's reign, hoping that I would get some facts regarding Sarmad, but it seems that political considerations have forced the writers to hold back their pen. I have scrutinised the events of 1070 AH, which is the year of Sarmad's martyrdom, in the hope that some mention might be found. It seems that great care had been taken to ensure that the blood of this martyr of Love did not stain the margins of the written page.

The year of Sarmad's martyrdom coincides with the annexation of Assam and Kuch Bihar by Aurangzeb. Granted that the conquest of Assam is no slight event, but little did the great general know that the eyes of the world, while not ignoring or diminishing this great victory, will forever shed tears on the sad defeat suffered by this lover of the Leila of Truth at his hands...

No one knows with clarity the truth about Sarmad's nationality or religion. Wali Daghestani writes that he was of Armenian origin. Other histories describe him as being Jewish. Wali Daghestani further adds that he was a native of Kashan. This idea is not farfetched because since ancient times, there have been Armenians living in Iran who though mainly Christians also have some Jews amongst them. Nowadays these people have adopted European culture and are ahead of all other Iranis in their acquisition of modern learning and science but a century ago, there was nothing except religion that distinguished them from the Muslims. Indeed, there were some amongst them who had acquired Muslim habits and customs and frequented the intellectual and cultural gatherings of the Muslims. Hence, we hear about many poets who were Armenian or

Christian, yet their verses were in no way inferior to the great Muslim poets of Iran. Whatever it may be, we know that Sarmad was of Armenian or Jewish origin and had embraced Islam in Iran; and like so many others he became part of the culture of Muslims so much so that he excelled them in the arts.

When the sun shines , it does not only search for the garden or flowers for its abode. Its generous bounty like that of God falls on all and sundry. If the golden cupolas of palaces glitter in its light, so do the dried and thorny branches of trees in the wilderness shine and bask in its glory. I am not talking of the sun which is the centre of our solar system but the sun of Islam. When the waves of this divine light rose, they washed away the extant distinctions based on race, blood and nation, like sticks and straws lying in their way. And when the time came of its blossoming, the freemen of Quraish, the slaves of Habsha, Mecca and Medina, The Franks and the inhabitants of Daghestan, Arab and non-Arab, the high and the low, the close and the distant, all were included in its bounty. Only merit and proficiency were the measure of rewards and each nation was given its fair share according to its ability. Bu Jahal was a Quraish and close to the Treasury, but he remained a pauper all his life. Bilal was a Habashi and Suhail a Rumi and far away, but they were blessed with wealth. The Blessed rain falls on all lands and they flower.

taufiq ba andaza-e himmat hai azal se
from eternity, rewards go to the deserving

aankhon mein hai woh qatra ke gauhar na hua tha.
the teardrop in the eye is worthy of a pearl.

It was due to this abundant generosity of Islam that Arabs, despite being at its centre, and birthplace, had no special position. The new Muslim races that came from far and distant lands excelled themselves in every branch of skill and learning so much so that Arabs had to make place for them in their midst, to the extent that if you were to look at the learned works of the times, there will be few indeed on which the non-Arab races have not left their mark. The point is that, just like the Love of God, the stint-less favour of Islam, was so universal that neither descent and nationality, nor colour and family played any role whatsoever. So too does the overflowing source of Divine Bounty remain on the lookout for those thirsting for Love: it has no business with lineage and nationality, with race or heredity. One example of this generous bounty is the story of Sarmad's life. He belonged to some Armenian family in Iran and was a Jew or Christian by religion. Early in his life the choice of Divine favour fell upon him and the attraction of mystical absorption and guidance drew him to the fold of Islam.

FAMILY NAME

We do not know what Sarmad's family name was, or what name he adopted on conversion to Islam. Generally, he has been referred to as only Sarmad. The truth is that Sarmad's anonymity should not surprise us because he belongs to the tribe of men whose first principle, nay whose pillar of faith, it is to be without name or token:

> *ba wajudat za man awaz niamad ke manam*
> given your existence, i did not find the voice to
> say 'i am…'

Some histories have referred to him as 'Syedai Sarmad'. We can deduce from this that part of his Muslim name was Syed. We know very little about his education, but the historians are united in the view that he was a highly learned and literate man.

PROFESSION

His early profession was trade, taking goods from Iran to India.

At the time, India was as much a centre of trade as it was of learning. But our young merchant, setting out for India, was unaware that when he arrived there, he would have to stake all his capital in the deal that awaited him. He was probably bringing in Irani goods to barter for the rubies and diamonds from Indian mines. But little did he know that fate had something else in store for him and he would end up trading till the end of his life! But not in marketplaces, where goods are bought and sold but in the bazaar of Beauty and Love, where instead of gold and silver, the currency is a broken heart and a wounded soul. And the trading is done by giving up one's peace of mind and emotional balance in exchange for a wayward glance or an indifferent air. And it is a reasonable price to pay for such precious ware.

sad milke dil ba neem nigah min tawan kharid
a hundred kingdoms of the heart can be bought
by half a glance

khoban dar in muamla taqsir mi kunand.
but the beautiful ones are negligent in this
matter.

And not just that, for that is only the outward show
of this bazaar. If courage allows you to walk further,
then you may have to make that final deal, the price
of which is no less than your life. And so, it happens
that life's overflowing cup transforms into the
overflowing goblet of martyrdom.

do alam naqd jan bar dast darand
the two worlds stand cash in hand

babazare ki saudae tu bashad.
in the bazaar where your love is sold.

In this period, Irani travellers used to come to
Hindustan via Sindh. Amongst the cities of Sindh,
Thatta was a prominent city but it has been relegated
to a mere name in modern times. This very Thatta
was that sacred Sinai, which became for Sarmad the

place of Divine revelation. And where the Laila of Beauty first unveiled her face to him. It is said that it was a Hindu boy whose infidel eyes had cast this spell.

This may not be farfetched for the needle of the quilt maker and the sword of the executioner are equal when it comes to rending the hearts of those who dwell in Love's abode. In this trade, the buyer is indifferent and uncaring while the seller concerned and eager. And then, those who carry their hearts like an offering in the palms of their hand, looking for a buyer, have no right to question who the buyer is and what qualities he has. It seems that this naïve and guileless Irani trader, tired of searching and stricken of heart, was looking desperately for a buyer; and when a buyer came, he did not even look up to see who it was and what was being offered. He considered it fortunate that he had found a beguiling eye which desired the cheap commodity of his heart and accepted the deal without a moment's hesitation.

dalal-e ishq bood kharidar-e janistan
the broker of love wanted to buy our life

khud ra farokhtaim cheh sauda ba ma raseed.
we sold ourselves, what a great deal we made!

This was for Sarmad the first step towards that wilderness in which he would be roaming in time to come. This is not just true for Sarmad alone.

Love by whatever name we call it, is that doorway through which man must pass before he can be truly human. A man who does not have passion in his soul or a tear in his eyes has no claim on humanity. Even the devout ascetic sitting in his hermitage, for all his stern abstinence cannot but do without the thought of the smiling *houris* of paradise. In other words, those dry characters who search for the Divine in the arches and alcoves of mosques cannot do without these imaginings.

hur-e jannat jalwa bar zahid dehad dar rahe dost
the *houris* of paradise reveal themselves to the
puritan on his path

andak andak ishq darkar avarad begana ra
slowly but surely, love is needed by those who
might stray.

17

This is why even those who search for Divine Truth have been seen to wander in the garden of the senses because if the heart is immune to the pleasures of suffering, it is a cube of ice that melts in water but is never seen to burn in fire. After all, to be human is to feel pain and sorrow and the cathedral of Love is a burning fire. Here only they can enter who are eager to sacrifice themselves at this flame and keep fanning it to ensure that the temperature keeps rising and the flame does not dim...

afsurda ra naseeb na bashad dile kabab
they are unfortunate who do not have their
hearts aflame

an yabad een nevala ke mahman aatish ast
they only receive this morsel who are the guests
of fire.

The first condition of loving the Divine is to turn away from worldly concerns but man is so chained and attached to earthly things that unless he receives a telling blow to the heart, he cannot break this link. When a bee alights on honey, it will only depart if it is shooed away. The human heart does not turn away from the pleasures of the world unless it is hurt. Only Love can deliver this incisive blow.

Only the angel of Love it is, who hides in his wings that powerful sword which can sever the ties that bind us to earthly pleasures and break the bonds of blood that restrict us. And when the heart is free of all restrictions and reflects upon itself, it finds no chains save the link of eternity that circles its feet. For this Love, wise Attar restlessly laments:

kufr kafir ra o din deedar ra
for the unbeliever unbelief, for the believer belief

zarra-e darde dile attar ra.
for Attar a particle of pain is enough.

Think about it: Anyone who is so dead of heart who has never had the good fortune of destroying his peace and sanity in anticipation of the unveiling of earthly beauty is hardly likely to experience the presence of Divine Beauty through his earthly senses.

That unfortunate one who has not spent his nights in longing for his earthly love is unlikely to be gifted with the yearning for the Divine Beloved.

That heartless one who has been unable to shower an indifferent and vain beloved with all his stability, pride and joy, heart and mind. Such a man is not likely to break the idol of self-worship and self-adoration that resides within him.

One who has not been driven crazy by the song of a beautiful creature is unlikely to be ecstatic when he hears the music of creation. Suffice it to say that he who is unfortunate enough never to lose his head and senses over a beauty's stark and unexpected gaze, will not be dizzy at the sight of the Divine. The wick that has been lit already will catch fire instantly whereas one which is new will take time to light up.

mohabbat ra dile gamdida ulfat beshtar geerad
those who have already suffered heartache are
quicker to fall in love

chirage ra ke dooday hast dar sarza dutar girad.
like the lamp which has already been lit is easier
to light again.

If the seekers are searching for beauty, then why wait for the hidden to be revealed? They should be startled and dazed by the light emanating from the veil. The lightless eyes did not wait for the presence of Yusuf. The smell of the garment was enough to awaken Jacobs's eyes.

That is why those who are gathered in the Tavern Of Truth are initially only served with a little wine and once the bitter drops are tolerated by the drinkers, only then does the *Saqi* unveil himself . Then there is no longer any need for the goblet or the wine. The glance of the wine giver itself is intoxicating enough for the drinker to lose himself in total abandon.

mai hajate neest mastaim ra
I don't need wine, i'm drunk on you

dar chashme tu ta khumar bashad
so long as your eyes are full of intoxication...

This very wine was placed before Sarmad and the quality of the wine rests to a great degree on the enticing hands of the wine-giver. So, we would not like to forget that Hindu boy, whose Laila like eyes turned Sarmad into a Majnun. But alas it is not the lot of every lover to be a Farhad or Qais. All we know of Sarmad's Laila was that it was a Hindu boy and when you consider it, it should be enough, for in the bazaar of Love, when a deal is struck one hardly cares who the buyer is and what the price!

mara farokht mohabbat valay nami danam
love has sold me and i am unaware

ki mushtari cheh kas ast o baha-e ma chand ast
who is the buyer and what the price!

There is even disagreement as to where this incident took place. Wali Daghestani writes that it happened at the port of Surat and Azad Bilgrami notes that it took place in Azimabad, Patna. But amongst all these *MIRATUL KHAYAL* is the oldest and it says, 'During his trading days, he came to Thatta and fell for a Hindu Boy'.

That is why we have preferred this version of events. The lightning may have struck anywhere for all that matters. We need to see what happened to the poor farmer's harvested grain.

Love's painful unsettling qualities are similar everywhere. Every lover may not be Qais but he certainly is a Majnun. And when Love arrives it demands that reason and good sense should leave and make room for it. Sarmad too suffered the same fate, and madness and absorption overtook him so much so that together with his reason and balance, he lost all his property and trading goods. The clothes on his body were the only chains that bound him to this world. Eventually, he was free of this burden too…because these limits are for those who are conscious. For the mad in love there are no such limits or obligations.

khata bamardume divana kas na mi girad
no one blames the mad for their lapses

junun na dari o aashufta khata inja ast
those who are sane, however, should be held responsible.

Desert Roaming is the tourism of the realm of love for it is through this that human reason becomes mature. 'Majnun' who is in the forefront of lovers is prominent because he has no equal in desert roaming. Sarmad too like Majnun before him,

23

roamed the desert and spent the hot and cold seasons of Hindustan in nakedness and was to discover that:

behuda chara dar talabash migardi
why do you roam uselessly in search of him

binashin agar ou khuda ast khud mi ayad
sit down – if he is god, he'll come himself.

And then he searched for a place to put love to its final test. But if this was the end then why all the roaming in the wilderness? But as I have stated myself, this too is included in the strange ways of love and in the laws of love:

ekay az dastigiri hai ishq ast
one way that love leads is

azizan ra bakhwari bar kasheedan.
to drag its friends into disrepute.

This was the time when Alamgir was to unleash a new game plan on India. It was the end of the Shahjahani era and Dara Shikoh was heir apparent. Dara Shikoh has been a unique figure in the Mughal Dynasty. And it is forever a matter of lament that his enemies controlled the pen with which the history of India was written. So, the real picture has been lost in the dust of political intrigue.

He was always a friend of ascetics and inclined towards mysticism and spent time in the company of *Sufis* and *Faqirs*. And some of his writings which have escaped plunder are witness to the fact that the writer was himself imbued with mystical experience and taste. The best proof that he was a man of such taste is that in his search for Truth he made no distinction between mosque and temple. The fervour with which he bowed before Muslim *Sufis* was matched by his devotion and respect for Hindu ascetics. Which Gnostic can disagree with this principle because if even in this state we were to distinguish between Belief and Unbelief, then what is the difference between those who know and those who are ignorant! The moth must seek the flame. If he only searches for it in the mosque, then his devotion to the flame is imperfect and wanting.

aashiq ham az islam kharab ast o ham az kufr
the lover cares not for Islam or *kufr*

parwana chirage haram o dayr na danad.
like the moth uncaring of the flame in temple or
mosque.

When Sarmad arrived at Shahjahanabad (Delhi) in this intoxicated state, fate stopped him there because the wine that he so craved was to be served in this tavern.

The poor man was uselessly banging his head against the argument between wisdom and madness. Little does he know that in this world there are scales on which if you put on one side 'madness' it will outweigh all the wisdom of the world on the other. And there are also such buyers that will sacrifice all their wealth of wisdom and balance for just an ounce of madness and would rush into the marketplace as if Joseph was on sale. Suffice it to say that we prefer Dara Shikoh's madness to the cunning wisdom of Aurangzeb because whereas the wise sword of Aurangzeb revels in the blood of those who yearn for Love, Dara's madness sacrifices itself and sheds its own blood. Maybe Dara Shikoh, weary of the cunning wisdom of the wise like Aurangzeb, had sought and preferred the company of madmen like Sarmad. Whatever the case, Sarmad began to spend

26

his time in the company of Dara Shikoh, who was also devoted to him. During this period, the anguish of love would sometimes force him to venture out, but since he knew that his final trial would be in Shahjahanabad, he remained there.

Eventually, Shah Jahan's illness and Dara Shikoh's vice regency brought forth Aurangzeb's secret plan and after a period of bloodletting and violence, Aurangzeb ascended the throne in 1069 AH. This period was as difficult for Dara Shikoh's companions as it was for him. Many of them made their escape with him. Those who remained found themselves in stormy waters. But Sarmad, lost in contemplation and absorption hardly had the time to look up and see what was going on around him. Because, despite his being oblivious of his surrounds, he was yet aware of the fact that whatever had happened in his life was only the initial stages of Love. The final test was still to come, and this is where it would happen.

bayak do zakhm ke khurdan za ishq bin mabash
don't think you're safe if you have received a
couple of blows in love

ke dar kameen gahe abroo kaman kash ast hanuz.
the archer is still there with many an arrow yet
hiding in those eyebrows.

Most historians have stated several reasons for Sarmad's martyrdom. The author of *MIRATUL KHAYAL* states that the robed doctors of the *Sharia* pricked up their ears at the following *rubai* (quatrain) of Sarmad's and they at once announced it as blasphemy as it was a denial of the *Miraj* (The Prophet's heavenly ascension).

har kas ke sirre haqiqatash pa dar shud
whosoever steps into the mystery of the true self

ou pahan taraz siphar pinha dar shud
encompasses the highest heavens

mulla goyad ke bar falak shud ahmad
the mulla says that Ahmad rose up to the
heavens

sarmad goyad falak ba ahmad dar shud.
Sarmad says the heavens came into Ahmad.

But what on earth had this guileless lover to do with legalistic battles? He was not even bothered enough to look up and take notice of the noise and commotion being created by these blind idiots. He was lost in a world so high that the clamorous noise of affirmation and denial could not even reach him.

dar ajaibhai ture- ishq hikmat ha kam ast
the wonders of the Sinai of love have little to do with logic

ishq ra ba maslehat andeshi-e majnun cheh kar.
love has little to do with reason and Majnun's schemes.

But the truth of the matter is that for Aurangzeb Sarmad's greatest crime was his association with Dara Shikoh and he wanted him killed under one pretext or another.

In Asia, politics has always operated under the guise of religion and thousands of murders committed for political ends have been hidden under religion's cloak. And when no valid pretext could be found, Sarmad was indicted for walking about naked and the *rubai* was quoted as evidence of his denial of the

Miraj of The Prophet. Mulla Qavi was the chief Qazi and he was dispatched by Aurangzeb to enquire the reason for his nakedness.

The Mulla asked Sarmad how, despite his being a learned and knowledgeable man, can he justify walking about unclad and revealing his private parts in public. Sarmad replied 'What can I do, *Shaitan* is QAVI (powerful) too'.

And then he spontaneously recited the following quatrain:

> *khush balai kardah chunin pust mara*
> I am humbled by a beautiful one

> *chashme bad-o-jaam burdah az dast mara*
> who has stolen my heart with his goblet eyes

> *ou dar baghal-e man ast o man dar talabash*
> he is by my side and I search everywhere for him

> *duzde ajabe birahna karda ast mara.*
> a strange robber has left me naked.

The Mulla turned angry and for good reason. Though Sarmad had not insulted Islam, the Mulla's own person had been made fun of, because his august name was ascribed to *Shaitan* the accursed. The Mulla promptly returned to Aurangzeb and reported that he found sufficient ground to prove Sarmad's unbelief.

He was about to take out his pen from his pen case. Is this not the scabbard where the bloodstained sword of these worldly doctors of the law resides? But Aurangzeb was far sighted enough to realise that such a pretext was not enough. He knew very well that Sarmad was not an ordinary man and his execution would not be just an everyday event. He was peerless in his knowledge and learning and was a popular figure amongst the multitude of Shahjahanabad. Therefore, it would not be politic to do anything till a proper and serious charge could be brought against him.

Throughout the 13 centuries of Islam, the pen of the jurists has been an unsheathed sword and the blood of thousands of truth seekers stains their *fatwas*. From whichever point you may like to study the history of Islam, you will find countless examples of when a ruler was intent on shedding blood, the pen of the jurist and the sword of the general rendered him equal service. This fate was not confined to *Sufis* and nobles alone; even orthodox scholars who dared to express the truth suffered at their hands and gave up their lives to escape their cruelty. Sarmad too was martyred by the same sword.

chun mi ravad naziri khunin kafan ba hashr
when Naziri arrives with bloodied shroud on judgement day

khalqe fughan kunand ke een dad khwah keest
all those assembled cry out 'who is this petitioner!'

Finally, it was decided that Sarmad should be brought before the learned scholars and jurists of the time and together they should reach a verdict.

Thus, an assembly was convened and Sarmad summoned before it. Aurangzeb himself addressed him first.

'People say that you, Sarmad had prophesied that Dara Shikoh would rule the kingdom? Is this true?

Sarmad replied:

'Yes, and my prophesy has been proved correct because Dara Shikoh was crowned as the ruler of the eternal kingdom.'

The turbaned doctors of the law then declared that going about naked was a violation of the *Sharia* and that no excuse for this is acceptable from someone of sound mind.

To this Sarmad had already given his answer:
duzday ajaby birahna karda ast mara
strange robber who has stripped me naked

Khalifa Ibrahim Badakshani was a renowned *Sufi* scholar who lived during the last days of Alamgir's reign. Wali Daghestani relates that according to him, when Sarmad was asked by the assembled scholars and jurists to put on clothes and he refused, the King intervened to say that mere nakedness cannot be treated as a capital offence and Sarmad should be asked to recite the *Kalima* (the Muslim profession of faith). He had asked for this because he had heard that one of Sarmad's idiosyncrasies was that he would only recite the first part of the *Kalima*; "I know no God..." and always omitted the second part which was "Save Allah". The Scholars then asked Sarmad to recite the *Kalima* and as was his habit he only recited the first part which was a negative statement. When the Ulema got excited and angry at this he retorted:

"I am absorbed in negation and have not reached the elevated stage of affirmation and if I say the rest i.e. There is no god save Allah, then I would be lying. And how can what is not in the heart, pass on the tongue?"

The Ulema instantly replied:

"To speak in such a manner is outright *kufr* (blasphemy). If you do not repent, you must be killed."

These worshippers of the superficial did not understand that Sarmad was far above listening to arguments about belief and unbelief and that he could not be cowed down by injunctions regarding killing and spilling of blood.

These *kufr*-obsessed, standing in the courtyard of mosque and *madrasah* may consider their throne to stand out at a considerable height; yet Sarmad stood on that minaret of Love, from which the walls of the Ka'ba and the Temple were of equal height and where the banners of Belief and Unbelief waved together:

kishaware hast ke dar way ravad az kufr sukhan
there is a world where the exponents of Unbelief have tread

hamah ja guft o shunow bar sare iman na ravad.
where the talk of Belief can hardly reach.

Sarmad had stated his position unambiguously. Those not content with belief in the unseen need confirmation of belief through a personal experience of the Truth. This was not yet granted to Sarmad. So why should he say something exists when he had not seen it or experienced it for himself? All those travelling in this realm have to pass through this station of doubt and negation but Sarmad's crime was to drink this cup in public whilst others do it privately. And he earned himself the censor's whip:

khirqa pooshan hama gar mast guzashtand guzasht
hidden by a cloak, the drinkers can pass by
unnoticed, drunk

qissa ma mast ke dar kuchao bazar bamand.
but the story of my drunkenness is spread on
every street.

Deeper reflection shows that this public declaration was necessary because if the final destination of this journey was martyrdom, then no matter which way he was going, he would be guided to the place where that could be achieved.

In short, when Sarmad did not repent, the Ulema without hesitation issued a *fatwa* for his execution and the next day he was taken to the execution ground. This happened in 1070 AH, barely a year after Aurangzeb ascended the throne.

When Sarmad was being taken to the execution ground, the whole city seemed to turn out and the streets were so crowded that walking through them became impossible. What can we say about the colourful story of Love, where the favoured spectacle is the shedding of blood and no sport more loved than martyrdom? When some martyr walks with pride to lay down his life, it seems a groom is riding in front of a wedding procession and the followers, the revellers.

bajurme ishq tu am mikashand gogha yast
the rumour is that I am being punished for loving you

tu niz barsare baam aa ke khush tamasha yast.
come and watch my love, it's a great spectacle.

But this was earthly love that requires spectators on the balcony otherwise Sarmad had no need even to raise his head.

When the executioner brandished his sword, Sarmad smiled, met his eyes, and said:

fidae tu shvam biya tu bahar surate ke mi ayee mun tora khub mi shinasam.
"i am sacrificed to you come! come! I recognize you full well whatever form you come in"

The writer of *MIRATUL KHAYAL* relates that after this sentence, Sarmad recited the following verse before placing head proudly on the block and gave up his life:

shuray shud o az khwabe adam chashm kashoodem
we opened our eyes from the dream of non-existence, hearing the clamour

didaym ke baqeest shabe fitna ghanoodem.
when we saw the night of sedition was not yet over, we slept again.

The author of *MIRATUL KHAYAL* was so busy in his sycophancy of Aurangzeb, that he could hardly spare the time to shed a tear at the Sarmad's blood soaked remains. But the unkindest cut of all is that he in his cold heartedness, ensured that this act of cruelty did not stain the volume containing the glorious deeds of Aurangzeb the pages of which as it happened were already coloured by enough blood.

You may also call this the vagary of Love that they whose hands are bloodied, in spite of being murderers and criminals, ask for blessings and praise; as if the garden of Love were also a playground of the beautiful who can shed blood and earn rewards.

Some people believe that Sarmad's remains are not in his tomb. Wali Daghestani, however confirms that he was buried there.

Even today, Sarmad's tomb is a place of pilgrimage for people from all walks of life and hands are still raised in prayer for him.

bar sare turbate man chun guzari himmat khwah
should you perchance upon my grave, take heart

ke ziarat gahe rindane jahan khwahad bud.
for this is a place of pilgrimage for the lovers of this world.

Aurangzeb ascended the throne in 1069 AH and Sarmad was martyred within a year of his rule, after which he reigned for over a decade. Some people think that

khunay ke ishq raizad hargiz badar na bashad
those who shed lovers' blood never find rest.

It was indeed the result of this bloody deed that during this whole period, Aurangzeb did not enjoy a moments rest or peace. To the extent that when his time came, he was in a state of poverty and distress. But the biographer must restrain his pen. When the blood of those who sacrificed themselves for love does not complain, then what right have we to raise our voice in anger.

When Sarmad himself said to his executioner, 'Come. I recognise you full well in any form you come in', then he could hardly hold any ill feelings towards Aurangzeb or his Ulema.

shud ast sina zahoori pur az mohabbate yaar
my soul, Zahoori, is brimming with love for my
beloved

barai keenah-e aghyar dar dilam ja neest.
there is no room in my heart for hatred of
others.

* Maulana Azad's introduction (in italics) has been slightly abridged.
Hayat-e-Sarmad. Lucknow, Tanvir, 1910.

Maulana Abul Kalam Muhiyuddin Azad
Sarmad the Martyr. London: Epicflo.com, 2006.

RUBAIYAT-E-SARMAD

1

Each sin illuminates your mercy O Lord

This is the reason for my sinful past O Lord

If sins are many, your forgiveness is even more

I saw this in many ways and in many forms O
Lord!

2

Each knot of meaning I have untied

None helped me in my need, how hard I tried!

True knowledge or justice I did not find

I looked hard and searched far and wide!

3

In the field of life's experiment I found

I had to deal with good and bad all around

But none listened to me save Thou

I searched in vain and naught I found.

4

O veiled one reveal Yourself and be,

I am searching endlessly for Thee;

My desire is to seek union with You

How long shall you hide from me?

5

Sarmad, what havoc on religion you have
bestowed

You've sacrificed belief for a pair of languid
eyes.

Having spent your life on *hadith,* and the Quran
divine

You went and to that idol worshipper your life
consigned!

6

Each one is after this world and hereafter

I seek freedom from both these imposters

Make me Yours, that is my only wish

Tear off the veil, reveal the secrets of hereafter!

7

In the breeze, I search your fragrance, my love

My eyes search the garden for your face, my
love

Alas! My heart and eyes are left wanting

Chance showed me the way to your street, my
love.

8

You have revealed your beauty to us

And showed us the way of loving you

Each eye with vision looks amazed at you

You reveal yourself in a hundred ways to us!

9

If you did not find love's infidelity

Nor love nor flower nor love's loyalty

You have not understood the secret

For both are in God's hand by god.

10

O Lord Thou art merciful, forgive me

Prove that my cry has reached Thee;

I am a sinner and yet am amazed how

Thou showers blessings on me.

11

Because of friends the garden was in spring

The taste for wine and love, and song

Alas, they passed away, the friends, the songs

When the sky toppled the glass of life's wine.

12

Beware dear heart fear not the enemy unkind

Cast out these useless thoughts from your mind

Why so caught up in the pleasure of this world

Beware, it's passing, all this desire, blind.

13

Death follows you in life, beware!

Your wealth and treasures will be lost, beware!

The struggle first, then only yearning for more

Desire for riches will make you poor, beware!

14

Sometimes he's kind, at other's indifferent, cruel

In various ways he shows himself to you

Embrace him with your sight and hold tight

Before this vision once again takes flight!

15

I am chaste, a Friend is all I need;

No rosary beads nor priestly girdle do I need

This robe of fake purity is full of deceit

To elevate my status, this I do not need.

16

Day and night, I dwell in impiety

My bowl and cup are full of sin

The world laughs and lifetime cries

At my purity, prayer and my fasting.

17

O Shaykh, it's best to drink this wine

Throw off your august robe, taste the divine;

Why call this blessing a forbidden crime

There is truth in it, drink up this wine!

18

Whoever abstains from wine is a fool;

Don't call him a man he is not wise;

Wine is another name for Love's pain,

It's the balm of broken hearts.

19

Each looked at the garden of life with greed

Some sought flowers and some thorns and
perished;

This life is a hidden mystery indeed

Learn from it O wise, take heed!

20

A man who is lost in lust and greed

Is sick in soul and always in need;

A hungry eye is never sated

Wherever I looked I saw this creed.

21

Wherever there is the pain of love there is rest,

He who has not this pain is dead at best.

Be not forgetful of wine and Love

If you want from this world what's best.

22

If someone gains, a little joy from you

That is a big gain and no loss to you;

Be not forgetful of this rare gift,

The river of life is full of sorrow too.

23

God is the Lord of good and bad,

None can deny this undeniable fact,

If you do not believe this then ask why,

Satan so powerful, and so weak, I?

24

He who unveils for you is a friend

He who spends all on you is a friend

You ask of Him and he gives freely,

He helps you when in need, a friend.

25

Not only the Ka'ba or the temple are His

The world and the heavens are His;

Why should not the world be mad for Him?

Wise is he who is enthralled by Him.

26

Not everyone knows the secret of love and wine;

Those dead of heart will never learn this truth
divine.

The Puritan has no clue of God or love

The ignorant can never know this wisdom fine!

27

Lover, love, idol, deceit, what are they?

Who knows this in Ka'ba and temple pray?

Come to the garden and the unity of colours see

Observe the lover, beloved, flower, thorn and
bee.

28

In self-worship, there is no gain O selfish one

If you aim so low, how will you scale the height?

You will gain nothing from this world when you
are done

You are full of loss, how can you gain O selfish
man.

29

Sarmad, the sorrow of love is not given to the
pleasure seeker

The burning of the moth is not given to the bee

It takes a lifetime for the Beloved to come in
your embrace

This wealth and fortune do not come to all and
sundry.

30

Your heart-winning ways are everywhere seen

Your kindness is in every aspect in every scene

I am a lover of your astonishing grace

You are behind the veil yet are everywhere to be
seen.

31

Each place of wine and pleasure of the garden

That is my abode, that is my home

It's meet you think me drunkard and a
worshipper of wine

Yet I take my place with the puritan and chaste.

32

The people of the world all yearn for wealth

No love or affection do they have at all

This fear you have for others is nothing

Fear those who are greedy one and all.

33

Each eyed the garden with desire, yearning

They took some flowers, thorns and went

This face of being is but a mystery unfolding

Pity the one who failed this to comprehend.

34

I looked up and saw the pleasures of the world
are gone

All that I worried about; all my treasure gone

All wealth that now remains with me

I must save, all chance of increasing it is gone!

35

Man who can be satisfied with a piece of bread,

Lives day and night in anxiety and dread

There is a storm raging in the ocean of life

Like a bubble his life, but he is still afraid.

36

The mystery of wine is not to everyone revealed

This secret from the dead of heart is oft
concealed

The Puritan knows not God, by god!

The ignorant can never flower in this field!

37

If you seek solace in this world unkind

Though on this earth peace is hard to find

Run away from people and find a place to hide

This is the only way to have peace of mind.

38

This body's day can easily turn to night

Any moment this piece of dry grass can be set
alight

O ignorant man there is no escaping death's
disaster

You a mere prisoner, remember the power of
your master.

39

Worrying about this brief life is futile

Seeking solace and pleasure in city or desert is
futile

Like a breeze each breath is coming and flowing
on

Every yearning for lasting desire and pleasure
futile.

40

My heart is always enthralled by my Beloved

Immersed in this fragrance, and the colours
divine

My heart's cup is filled with this wine

Whatever is in this goblet reflects this Friend of
mine.

41

My heart is caught in love's trap again

My thoughts drift to the beloved once again

I am old and my heart is feeling young

In autumn I feel the rush of youthful spring
again.

42

In youth, Satan failed to seduce me

My cloak was never soiled by the dust of sin

As I grow old, I turn to sinful thoughts

It is a pain for which there's no remedy.

43

Alas my friends have all gone beneath the earth

Trampled down by the onward march of time

They rose to heights and roamed the skies

Now lie in dust each one of them.

44

Alas I never reached the depths of Truth

I tried and tried but it was all in vain

Bewildered that I could never reach or find

The one who wove the spider's web in my
mind.

45

Each one in this world is after a loaf of bread

There is no friend that I can call a friend of mine

Each roams the street like a dog after a morsel

Strange ways of friendship in this world I've
seen.

46

Instead of examining another's qualities and
faults,

Look at your own heart and yourself within

This is the best way to dwell in this world

Do not dwell on other people's sins.

47

He who embraced Him in his mind

Is not mad, he's sane

The feeling of this intoxicant is divine

More powerful than any wine!

48

I was given the highest rank by love

It made me from other's favours free

Like a lamp in the gathering I burned

So much that I became one with the Mystery.

49

Though he is aware of all my faults and sins

He never turns his blessings away from me

However much I fear and lose hope

I always find him full of Mercy.

50

O Lord, I cannot reach out to anyone

All hope is gone, I am alone

Like a prisoner in this world I feel

Only your blessings can my suffering heal.

APPENDIX

RUBAIYAT-E-SARMAD

Farsi and Transliteration

1

از جرم فزوں یافته ام فضل ترا

اینں شد سبب معصیت بیش مرا

ہر چند گنہ بیش کرم بیشتر است

دیدم ہمہ جا وٰ آزمودم ہمہ را

Az jurm fuzun yafta-am fazl tora

Een shud sabab-e masiyat-e besh mara

Har chand gunah besh karam beshtar ast

Deedam hama ja o aazmoodam hama ra

2

از کار جہاں عقدہ کشودم ہمہ را

در محنت و اندوہ ربودم ہمہ را

حق دانی و انصاف ندیدم زکسے

دیدم ہمہ را و آواز مودم ہمہ را

Az kar-e-jahan uqda kashoodam hama ra

Dar mehnat o andoh raboodam hama ra

Haq dani o insaaf na deedam za kase

Deedam hama ra o awazmoodam hama ra

3

در بادئیہ تجربہ یا رب ہمہ جا

افتاد و سرو کار بہ زشت و زیبا

غیر از تو کسے نہ گشت فریاد رسم

دیدم ہمہ را و ازمودم ہمہ را

Dar badiyah tajurba – Ya Rub! hama ja
Uftad sar o kar ba zisht o saba
Ghair az to kase na gashte faryad rasam
Deedam hama ra o azmoodam hama ra

4

اے جلوہ گر نہاں عیاں شوبد را

در فکر بجستیم کہ ہستی تو کجا

خواہم کہ در آغوش کنارت گیرم

تا چند تو در پردہ نمائی خود را

Aye jalwagar nihan-ayaan shobad raa
Dar fikr e bajasteem ke hasti tu kuja
Khawaham ke dar aghosh e kinarat geeram
Ta chand tu dar e parda numai khud ra

96

5

سرمد در دیں عجب شکستے کردی
ایماں بہ فدائ چشم مستے کردی
عمرے کے بآیات و احادیث گڈشست
رفتی و نثار بت پرستے کردی

Sarmad dar e deen ajab shikaste kardi
Imaan ba fidai chashm e maste kardi
Umre ke ba ayat o ahadith guzasht
Rafti o nisar e butt paraste kardi

6

شادی بود از دین و ز دنیا ہمہ را
از ہر دو نجات دہ کہ شادیست مرا
آشفتئہ خود مکن کہ آنم ہوس است
از پردہ بروں آئی و خود را بنما

Shadi bu'ad as deen o ze dunya hama ra
Az har do najaat deh ke shaadeest mara
Ashufta khud makun ke aanam havas ast
Az parda barun aye o khud ra benuma

از باد صبا خواست دلم بوئے ترا
چشمم ز چمن جست گل روئے ترا
آخر نہ ازیں دوچار گشتے نہ از آن
اندیشہ نشاں داد رہ کوئے ترا

Az baad e saba khwast dilum boo-e tora
Chashmam ze chaman joost gul e roo- e tora
Aakhir na azeen duchaar gashte na azaan
Andesha Nishan daad rah e koo e tora

8

کردی تو علم بر لربائی خود را
ہم در فن و مہر آشنائی خود را
ایں دیدہ کہ بیناست تماشائی تست
ہر لحضہ بصد رنگ نمائی خود را

Kardi to alam ba dilrubai khud ra
Ham dar fan o mehr aashnai khud ra
Een deeda ke beenast tamashi e tust
Har lahza ba sad rang numai khud ra

9

ہر جا کہ نیابی تو نشانے ز جفا

یا مہر و محبت گل و بوئے ز وفا

از خلق و ز خلق خود ندانی ہر گز

آں ہر دو بدست اوست گفتم بخدا

Har ja ke niabi tu nishaan-e ze jafa
Ya mehr o muhabbat gul o bu-e zewafa
Az khalq o ze khulq khud na dani hargiz
Aan har do badast oost guftam ba khuda

10

یا رب ز کرم بخشش تقصیر مرا

مقبول بکن نالۂ شبگیر مرا

ما پر ز گناہ ماجرائیست عجیب

لطف تو کند چارۂ تدبیر مرا

Ya Rub ze karam bakhshish taqseer mara
Maqbool ba kun nala e shabgeer mara
Ma pur ze gunah majra eest ajeeb
Lutf e tu kunad chara e tadbeer mara

11

از صحبتِ هَمدمان به باغ و صحرا

ذوقِ سخنی بودو هوای مینا

آخر سخنی ماند و عزیزان رفتند

مینائ فلک فگَند او را از پا

Az suhbat e hamdaman ba baagh o sahra

Zauq e sukhan e bood o huva e meena

Aakhir sukhan e maand o azizan raftand

Mina-e falak figand oo ra az paa

12

باز آ باز آ ز فکر باطِل باز آ

از وهم و خیال خام ای دل باز آ

خشنود مشو ز فکر دُنیا هرگز

نه وصل نماید و نه واصل باز آ

Baz aa baaz aa ze fikr-e-baatil baz aa

Az wahm o khayal e kham aye dil baz aa

Khushnood mashoo ze fikr e dunya hargiz

Na wasl numayad o na wasil baz aa

13

مرگ است در این بادیه دنبال ترا

اینست مآل کار از مال ترا

اول محنت و آخرش حسرت هست

این مال کند همیشه پا مال ترا

Marg ast dar een badiya danbal tora

Eenast m'al kar az maal tora

Avval mehnat o akhirash hasrat hast

Een maal kunad hamesha pamaal tora

14

گه مهر و وفا کند گهی ناز و جفا

هر لحظه به صد رنگ نماید خود را

آغوش نظر گشا که آید به کنار

یک گام نگردد ز تو پیوسته جدا

Gahe mehr o wafa kunad gah naaz o jafa

Har lahza ba sadrang numayad khud ra

Aagosh nazar kusha ke ayad ba kinaar

Yek gaam ngardad ze tu pewasta juda

15

گر متقیم کار به یار است مرا

با سجه و زنار کار چه کار است مرا

این خرقه پشمینه که صد فتنه دروست

بازش نکشم به دوش عار است مرا

Gar mutaqqayam kar ba yaar ast mara

Ba subbah o zunnar che kaar ast mara

Een khirqa e pashmina ke sad fitna duroost

Bazash na kasham ba dosh aar ast mara

16

این فسق و فجور کارِ هر روزه ی ما

پُر شد ز گناه کاسه و کوزه ما

میخندد روزگار و میگرید عمر

بر طاعت و بر نماز و بر روزه ما

Een fisq o fujur kaar e har rozah-e-ma

Pur shud ze gunah kasa o kuza-e ma

Mi khandad rozgar o mi giryad umr

Bar ta'at o bar namaz o ba roza-e ma

17

زاهد تو بخور باده که بسیار نکوست
از خرقه کِشی خمار صد فتنه دروست
بی شبهه حلال است بگوئی تو حرام
کیفیت این هر که بیاید همه اوست

Zahid tu bekhor bada' ke bisyar nakoost
Az khirqa kushy khumar sad fitna duroost
Be shubha halal ast begoi tu haram
Kaifiyat e een har kebiyayad hama oost

18

هر کس که ز می توبه کند نادان است
انسان نتوان گفت بگو حیوان است
این سلسله جنبانِ غمِ جانان است
هر آتش افسرده ولی دامان است

Har kas ke za mai tauba kunad nadan ast
Insaan na tavaan guft bego haivan ast
Een silsila junbaan-e-gham-e janan ast
Har aatish-e afsurda dili daman ast

19

هر کس بهوس باغ جهان دید گزشت

خار و گل پژ مرده بهم چید گزشت

این صورت هستی که تمامش معنی است

افسوس بر آنکس که نه فهمید گزشت

Har kas ba havas bagh-e-jahan deed guzasht

Khar o gul e paz marda baham cheed guzasht

Een surat-e hasti ke tamamash ma'ni ast

Afsos bar aankas ken a fahmmed guzasht

20

آنرا که هوس بیش بود آزار است

از شربت دنیا رویش بیمار است

از گرسنه چشمی به جهان سیری نیست

این طائفه دیدم همه جا بسیار است

Aan ra ke havas besh buvad aazar ast

Az sharbat e dinar o dilash bimar ast

Az gar siyah chashmi ba jahan sairi neest

Een taifa deedam hama ja bisyar ast

21

هر جا که غمِ یار بود آرام است

بی این بجهان هر که بود ناکام است

غافل نشوی ز یار و از باده ی ناب

گر دولتِ جم می طلبی با جام است

Har ja ke gham e yaar buvad aaram ast

Be een ba jahan har ke buvad nakaam ast

Ghafil na shavi ze yaar o az bada'e naab

Gar daulat-e jam mi talabi ba jam ast

22

نفعی بکسی اگر رسانی هنر است

سود است درین سود بخود بیشتر است

زین گوهر نایاب نگردی غافل

این بحر پُر آشوب جهان در گذر است

Nafa e ba kase agar rasani hunar ast

Saudaast dar een sood bakhud beshtar ast

Zeen gauhar e nayab na gardi ghafil

Een bahr e pur ashob jahan dar guzar ast

23

هر نیک و بدی که هست در دست خداست

این معنی پیدا و نهان در همه جاست

باور نکنی گر درینجا بنگر

این ضعف من و قوتِ شیطان ز کجا است

Har nek o baday ke hast dar dast-e khuda ast
Een ma'ni paida o nehan dar hama ja ast
Bawar na kuni gar dar eenja benigar
Een zauf e man o quwat e Shaitan ze kuja ast

24

بی سر و قدی که رو نماید یار است

بی سیمبری که زر رباید یار است

آن یار گزین که هر چه خواهی بدهد

یاری که بکارِ تو بیاید یار است

Be sarv o qade ke roonumayad yaar ast
Be seembare ke zar rubayad yaar ast
Aaan yaar gazin ke har che khwahi be dehad
Yaare ke bakar-e tu beyayed yaar ast

25

تنها نه همین دیر و حرم خانه اوست
این ارض و سما تمام کاشانه اوست
عالم همه دیوانه افسانه اوست
عاقل بود آن کسی که دیوانه اوست

Tanha nah hameen dayr o haram khana-e oost
Een arz o sama tamam kashana- e oost
Alam hama divana-e afsana-e oost
Aaqil buvad aan kas yake divana-e oost

26

اسرار می و جام به کس روشن نیست
این راز بهر مرده دلی گفتن نیست
زاهد بخدا که از خدا بیخبری
سر رشته این به دست هر کودن نیست

Asrar e mai-o-jaam ba kas raushan neest
Een raz ba har murda-dile guftan neest
Zahid ba khuda ke az khuda bekhabari
Sar rishta e een ba dast har koodan neest

27

عاشق و عشق و بت و بتگر و عیاری نیست
کعبه و دِیر و مساجد همه جا تاریکیست
گر در آئی به چمن وحدت یکرنگی بین
غور کن عاشق و معشوق و گل و خار یکیست

Ashiq o ishq o butt o buttgar o ayyare keest
Ka'ba o dayr o masajid hama ja tareek eest
Gar dar aaiy ba chaman wahdat e yak rangi been
Ghaur kun aashiq o mashooq o gul o khare keest

آسوده دمی ز خود پسندی مطلب
زین همتِ پستِ خود بلندی مطلب
سودای جهان سود ندارد چندان
نقصان بپذیر سودمندی مطلب

Aasooda dam-e ze khud pasandi matlab
Zeen himmat e past e khud bulandi matlab
Sauda e jahan sood na darad chandan
Nuqsan ba zer e sood mandi matlab

29

سرمد غم عشق بوالهوس را ندهند

سوزِ دل پروانه مگس را ندهند

عمری باید که یار آید به کنار

این دولت سرمد همه کس را ندهند

Sarmad gham e ishq bul havas ra na dihand
Soz-e-dil-e parvana magas ra na dihand
Umre bayad ke yaar ayad ba kinaar
Een daulat-e Sarmad hama kas ran na dihand

30

مشهور شدی به دلربائی همه جا

بتمثیل شدی در آشنائی همه جا

من عاشق این طور توام می بینم

خود را ننمائی و نمائی همه جا

Mash-hoor shudi ba dilrubai hama ja
Be misl shudi dar ashnai hama ja
Man aashiq e een taur tu am mi beenam
Khud ran na numai o numai hama ja

31

هر جا که گِلِ اياغِ جوشِ چمن است
او مسکن دل خوش است ما را وطن است
گر باده پرست مست گوئی حق است
ور زاهد متقی بگوئی سخن است

Har ja ke gil e ayagh josh e chaman ast
Oo maskan e dil khush ast mara watan ast
Gar bada parast mast goi haq ast
Dar Zahid e muttaqi beh goi sukhan ast

32

دنيا طالبان را که غمِ دنيار است
بمهری شان بيکدگرِ بسيار است
از عقرب و و مار هيچ انديشه مکن
زين قوم حذر بِکن. که نيش و خار است

Dunya talaban ra ke gham e deenar ast
Be mehri shan ba yekdeegar bisyaar ast
Az aqrab o mar heech andhesha makun
Zeen qawm hazr bakun ke neesh o khaar ast

33

هر کس بهوس باغ جهان دید گذشت
خار و گل پژمرده بهم چید گذشت
این صورت هستی که تمامش معنی است
افسوس بر آن کس که نفهمید گذشت

Har kas ba havas bagh e jahan deed guzasht
Khar o gul e paz marda baham cheed guzasht
Een surat e hasti ke tamamash ma'ni ast
Afsoos bar aan kas ke na fahmeed guzasht

34

دیدی که غم و عیش جهان زود گذشت
چیزیکه در اندیشه تو بود گذشت
این یک دو نفس که ماند سرمایه تو
هشیار که نقصان نکنی سود گذشت

Deedi ke gham o aish jahan zood guzasht
Cheeze ke dar andesha e tu bood guzasht
Een yek do nafas ke maand sarmaya e tu
Hushyaar ke nuqsan na kuni sood guzasht

35

انسان که شکم سیری از یک نان است

از حرص و هوا شام و سحر نالان است

در بحر وجودش بنگر طوفان است

اخرچو حباب یک نفس مهمان است

Insaan ke shikam seri az yak nan ast

Az hirs o hava sham o sahar nalan ast

Dar behr e wujudash binigar tufaan ast

Aakhir chu habab yak nafas e mehman ast

36

اسرار می و جام به کس روشن نیست

این راز بهر مرده دلی گفتن نیست

زاهد بخدا که از خدا بیخبری

سر رشته این بدست هر کودن نیست

Asrar e mai o jam ba kas raushan neest

Een raaz bahar murda dile guftan neest

Zahid ba khuda ke az be khabari

Sar rishta e een ba dast har koodan neest

37

خواهی نکشی رنج دنیا بی زحمت

از مردم روزگار بگزین عزلت

هر چند که بر روی زمین راحت نیست

گر هست همین است بدنیا راحت

Khwahi na kushi ranj dunia be zahmat
Az mardum e rozgar bagazin uzlat
Har chand ke bar roo-e-zameen rahat neest
Gar hast hameen ast ba duniya rahat

38

این جسم به صد قسم فنا بنیاد است

این شعله حس در نفسی بر باد است

از دامِ اجل ترا رهائی نبود

صیدی و سر و کار تو با صیاد است

Een jism ba sad qism fana bunyad ast
Een shula e hiss dar nafase barbad ast
Az daam e ajal tora rihai na buvad
Sai'di o sar o kar-e to ba Sayyad ast

39

از بهر دو روز فکر دنیا غلط است

دل بستن معموره و صحرا غلط است

مانند نسیم هر نفس در گذری

این حرص و هوا و این تمنا غلط است

Az bahr e do roz fikre duniya ghalat ast
Dil bastan e ma'moora-o sahra ghalat ast
Manind e naseem har nafas-e dar guzri
Een hirs o hava o een tamana ghalat ast

40

وارسته دلم همیشه وابسته اوست

پیوسته درین باغ به رنگ گل و بوست

لبریز محبّت است مینای دلم

از کوزه همان برون تراود که دروست

Warasta dilam hameesha wabasta-e- oost
Pewasta dar een bagh ba range gul o boost
Labrez-e mohabbat asat minai dilam
Az kooza haman beroon taravud ke duroost

41

دل باز گرفتارِ نگاری شده است
از فکر و غمِ لاله عذاری شده است
من پیر و دلم ذوقِ جوانی دارد
هنگامِ خزان جوش بهاری شده است

Dil baaz giraftar-e nigare shudah ast
Az fikr o ghame lala azaare shudah ast
Man pir o dilam zauq e jawani darad
Hangam e khizaan josh- e bahare shudah ast

42

ایام شباب زور شیطان نرسید
بر دامنِ من غبارِ عصیان نرسید
پیری چو رسید معصیت گشتِ جوان
دردی عجبی رسید و درمان نرسید

Ayyam e Shabab zor- e Shaitan na raseed
Bar daman-e-man ghubar-e isyaan na raseed
Peeri chu raseed ma'siyat e gasht-e jawaan
Darday ajabay raseed o darmaan na raseed

43

بنگر که عزیزانِ همه در خاک شدند
در صید گهِ فنا بفتراک شدند
آخر همه را خاک نشین باید شد
گیرم که برفعت همه افلاک شدند

Benigar ke azizaan hama dar khak shudand
Dar sayd gahe fana ba fitrak shudand
Aakhir hama ra khak nasheen bayad shud
Geeram ke ba raf'at hama aflak shudand

44

افسوس که کنهش بخیالم نرسید
اندیشه درین بادیه بسیار دوید
بر روی خیالِ خامِ حیران شده ام
بر پردهِ عنکبوت صورت که کشید

Afsos ke kuhnash ba khyalum na raseed
Andesha dar een baad ya bisyaar daveed
Bar roo-e khyal e khaam hairan shudah am
Bar parda-e ankabut surat ke kasheed

45

هر کس پی نانی بجهان دوست بود
یک دوست ندیدیم ز جان دوست بود
چون سگ ز پی لقمه بهر در بدوند
اینست نشان که نامِ نشان دوست بود

Har kas pa-e nan-e ba jahan dost bu'ad
Yek dost na deedaim ze jaan dost bu'ad
Chun sag ze pa-e luqma ba har dar badavand
Eenast nishaan ke naam e nishaan dost bu'ad

46

هر گاه به بینی زکسے عیب و هنر
عیب و هنر خویش در آور به نظر
این است هنر بهتر از ین نیست دگر
خود را بنگر بعیب مردم منگر

Har gah ba beeni za kasay ayb o hunar
Ayb o hunar e khwesh dar aawar beh nazar
Een ast hunar behtar az een neest digar
Khud ra binigar ba ayb mardam minigar

47

هر کس بیخیال او هم آغوش بود
دیوانه نماید همه سر هوش بود
کیفیت این نشه بکس ظاهر نیست
این باده نهان همیشه در جوش بود

Har kas ba khayaale oo ham-agosh bu'ad
Divana numayad hama sar hosh bu'ad
Kaifiyat-e een nashah ba kas zahir neest
Een bada nihaan hameesha dar josh bu'ad

48

از منصب عشق سرافرازم کردند
وز منّتِ خلق بی نیازم کردند
چون شمع درین بزم گدازم کردند
از سوختگیِ محرمِ رازم کردند

Az mansab e ishq sarfarazam kar dand
Waz minnat-e khalq be niazam kar dand
Chun sham'a dar een bazm gudazam kar dand
Az sokhtagi mahram-e razam kar dand

49

هر چند که عصیانِ مرا می داند

بر خوانِ هر نفسی می خواند

در خوف و رجا بسی تاَمّل کردم

بیش از همه مائل بکرم می ماند

Har chand ke isyaan-e mara mi danad
Bar khwan e karam har nafase mi khwanad
Dar khauf o rija basay ta'ammul kar dam
Besh az hama mayal ba karam mi maenad

50

یا رب بکسی مرا رسانی نبود

امید وفا ز آشنائی نبود

در دایره ی تجربه پا بند شد

غیر از درِ رحمّت رهائی نبود

Ya Rub ba kase mara rasai na bu'ad
Umeed-e wafa o aashnai na bu'ad
Dar daira-e tajurba paband shudam
Ghair az dar-e rahmat rehai na bu'ad

Made in the USA
Middletown, DE
22 January 2022

59424307R00078